HOME CANNING

AND PRESERVING

TABLE OF CONTENTS

INTRODUCTION

In a world where convenience often reigns supreme, the art and science of home canning and preserving stand as enduring traditions, offering not only a delightful journey into the culinary realm but also a profound gateway to sustainable living and food security. At its essence, home canning and preserving epitomize the harmonious union of time-honored techniques and modern-day necessity, allowing us to capture the bounty of nature's harvest and savor its richness long after the season has passed.

The art of canning and preserving is far more than a simple act of extending the shelf life of food; it's a tribute to resourcefulness, a celebration of flavors, and a commitment to reducing waste while embracing the wholesome essence of natural produce. Its purpose is rooted in the preservation of seasonal abundance, transforming fleeting moments of plenty into year-round sustenance. This practice not only ensures a steady supply of nourishment but also cultivates a deeper connection with the food we consume and the environment that sustains us.

At its core, home canning and preserving are acts of sustainability. By harnessing fresh produce at its peak and preventing spoilage, we reduce food waste and contribute to a more sustainable food ecosystem. By preserving fruits, vegetables, and other ingredients at their freshest, we retain their nutritional value, ensuring a pantry stocked with wholesome, vitamin-rich foods devoid of artificial preservatives.

Home canning offers a cost-effective means of enjoying high-quality, organic produce year-round without succumbing to the fluctuating prices of out-of-season fruits and vegetables. Canning and preserving allow for the preservation of flavors unique to each harvest. Moreover, it empowers us to craft custom blends, preserves, and pickles, tailored to personal preferences and dietary needs.

In an era marked by unpredictability, home canning provides a sense of security by creating a reserve of sustenance, lessening dependence on store-bought goods, especially during shortages or emergencies. This time-honored practice bridges generations, preserving culinary heritage and passing down invaluable knowledge, fostering a sense of community and familial ties.

In this guide to home canning and preserving, we embark on an illuminating journey into the heart of this time-honored tradition. From mastering the art of safe canning techniques to exploring various preservation methods, recipes, and troubleshooting, this guide endeavors to equip you with the knowledge, confidence, and inspiration to embark on your own fulfilling and rewarding preservation journey.

Through meticulous attention to safety guidelines, detailed step-by-step instructions, and a celebration of the diverse array of flavors and possibilities, this guide aspires to empower you to transform seasonal abundance into jars of delectable goodness that will grace your tables and enliven your meals throughout the year.

Join us as we delve into the fascinating world of home canning and preserving, where the beauty of nature's harvest meets the ingenuity of human craftsmanship to create a tapestry of flavors and nourishment that transcends seasons.

CHAPTER ONE

WHAT IS HOME CANNING AND PRESERVING?

Home canning and preserving are time-honored food preservation techniques aimed at extending the shelf life of fresh produce, allowing it to be stored and consumed well beyond its harvest season. These methods involve capturing the goodness of seasonal fruits, vegetables, and other perishable foods at their peak freshness and flavor, sealing them in containers (such as glass jars or cans), and using various preservation techniques to prevent spoilage.

Home Canning:

• Water Bath Canning: This method is suitable for high-acid foods like fruits, tomatoes, pickles, and jams. It involves submerging sealed jars in boiling water to create a vacuum seal, preventing the growth of bacteria, yeast, and molds.

• Pressure Canning: This method is necessary for low-acid foods like meats, vegetables, and some fruits. Pressure canning uses a specialized pressure canner to heat food at a higher temperature than boiling water, eliminating harmful microorganisms like Clostridium botulinum that thrive in low-acid environments.

Preserving Techniques:

Apart from canning, there are various other preserving methods:

• Pickling: This involves submerging food in a solution of vinegar, salt, and spices. The acidity of the vinegar prevents spoilage and adds a tangy flavor to vegetables like cucumbers, beets, or peppers.

• Jam and Jelly Making: Cooking fruits with sugar and pectin, then sealing them in jars, creates jams, jellies, and preserves. The high sugar content acts as a preservative, and the heat and sealing process prevent microbial growth.

• Fermentation: This process involves using beneficial bacteria to preserve food. Vegetables like cabbage in sauerkraut or cucumbers in pickles undergo fermentation, which not only preserves them but also introduces unique flavors.

• Dehydration: Removing moisture from food through drying prevents the growth of bacteria and mold. Fruits, vegetables, and herbs can be dehydrated using specialized equipment or even sunlight.

Why Home Canning and Preserving?

• Health and Nutrition: Preserving food at home ensures control over ingredients, limiting additives and preservatives. It retains the nutritional value of fresh produce, providing healthier alternatives to store-bought options.

• Reducing Food Waste: These methods help in utilizing excess produce that might otherwise go to waste, promoting sustainable practices and reducing the carbon footprint.

• Cost-Effectiveness: By preserving surplus fruits and vegetables at their peak, individuals can enjoy high-quality, locally sourced produce throughout the year without relying on expensive store-bought items.

• Self-Sufficiency and Preparedness: Home canning provides a sense of self-sufficiency, enabling individuals to create a pantry stocked with homemade goods, which can be especially valuable during emergencies or times of scarcity.

Home canning and preserving are not only practical skills but also traditions that connect us with the bounty of nature, fostering creativity in the kitchen while preserving the flavors and essence of seasonal produce for year-round enjoyment.

THE PURPOSE AND BENEFITS OF HOME CANNING AND PRESERVING.

Home canning and preserving serve multiple purposes and offer numerous benefits that contribute to healthier, sustainable, and more cost-effective lifestyles. Here's a detailed breakdown:

Purpose of Home Canning and Preserving:

• Food Preservation: The primary purpose is to extend the shelf life of seasonal fruits, vegetables, and other perishable foods beyond their harvest period. By utilizing various preservation methods, such as canning, pickling, fermenting, and dehydrating, these foods can be stored for extended periods while retaining their flavor, nutrients, and quality.

• Reducing Food Waste: Canning and preserving allow individuals to utilize surplus or excess produce that might otherwise spoil or go to waste. This reduces food waste at home and contributes to a more sustainable food system.

• Creating Shelf-Stable Pantry Items: These techniques transform perishable goods into shelf-stable pantry items, providing a readily available supply of preserved foods throughout the year. This ensures a constant source of nutritious and flavorful ingredients for meals.

Benefits of Home Canning and Preserving:

• Nutritional Retention: Home canning involves preserving foods at their peak freshness, locking in essential vitamins, minerals, and nutrients. This ensures that preserved foods maintain their nutritional value, often surpassing store-bought alternatives that might contain preservatives or lose nutrients during long-term storage.

• Healthier Eating Options: Homemade canned and preserved foods typically contain fewer additives, artificial colors, and preservatives than commercially processed goods. Individuals have greater control over ingredients, allowing for healthier eating choices tailored to personal dietary preferences and restrictions.

• Cost-Effectiveness: Preserving surplus produce from gardens or local markets during peak seasons can significantly reduce grocery expenses throughout the year. It allows individuals to enjoy high-quality, organic, and locally sourced foods at a fraction of the cost of store-bought equivalents.

• Sustainability and Reduced Environmental Impact: By preventing food waste and relying on homegrown or locally sourced ingredients, home canning and preserving contribute to sustainable living practices. This reduces the environmental impact associated with transportation, packaging, and the disposal of excess food.

• Food Security and Preparedness: Having a well-stocked pantry of preserved foods offers a sense of security during emergencies, natural disasters, or times of scarcity. It promotes self-sufficiency and preparedness by providing access to nourishing foods when fresh produce might not be readily available.

• Culinary Creativity and Flavor Diversity: Home preservation methods open doors to experimentation with flavors, allowing individuals to create custom blends, unique pickles, jams, or fermented products. It fosters creativity in the kitchen and introduces diverse flavors and textures to meals.

In essence, home canning and preserving are not just practical skills; they represent a holistic approach to food, emphasizing sustainability, health, self-sufficiency, and culinary creativity while connecting individuals to the tradition of preserving the harvest for year-round enjoyment.

THE IMPORTANCE OF SAFETY MEASURES

Safety measures in home canning and preserving are paramount to ensure the prevention of foodborne illnesses, maintain food quality, and guarantee the long-term safety of preserved goods. Emphasizing these safety measures is crucial to safeguarding the health of those consuming home-canned foods. Here's a detailed explanation highlighting their importance:

1. Prevention of Foodborne Illnesses:

Botulism Risk: Improperly canned or preserved foods can create an environment conducive to the growth of Clostridium botulinum, a bacterium that produces a deadly toxin causing botulism. Adequate safety measures prevent the growth of this bacterium, ensuring food safety.

Bacterial Contamination: Any breach in canning or preserving techniques, such as using unclean equipment or improper sealing, can lead to bacterial contamination. This can result in illnesses like salmonella, E. coli, or listeriosis if consumed.

2. Ensuring Long-Term Safety:

Seal Integrity: Proper sealing of jars or containers is crucial to creating a vacuum that prevents the entry of air and microorganisms. This maintains the integrity of the seal, preserving food quality and preventing spoilage.

Acidification and Heat Treatment: Acidification (for water bath canning) and adequate heat treatment (for pressure canning) destroy bacteria, molds, and yeasts, ensuring that preserved foods remain safe for consumption over time.

3. Quality Maintenance:

Texture and Flavor: Adhering to safety guidelines ensures that the texture, flavor, and overall quality of preserved foods are maintained. Improperly processed or stored foods may lose taste, color, or texture due to spoilage.

Storage Conditions: Following safety protocols regarding proper storage conditions, such as cool, dark spaces for canned goods, helps maintain their quality and prolong shelf life.

4. Importance of Guidelines and Standards:

Reputable Sources: Adhering to guidelines provided by trusted sources like the USDA, National Center for Home Food Preservation, or local extension offices ensures reliable information and safe practices.

Updated Information: Continuously staying informed about the latest safety recommendations, techniques, and best practices ensures that the preservation methods align with current safety standards.

5. Responsibility to Consumers:

Protecting Consumers: As a preserver, you hold responsibility for the safety of the products you distribute or share. Prioritizing safety measures safeguards the health of those consuming your preserved goods.

Educating Others: Promoting safety measures when sharing knowledge about home canning and preserving helps educate others on the importance of these practices for their health and well-being.

In summary, emphasizing safety measures in home canning and preserving is not just a recommended practice; it's an ethical responsibility. It ensures the prevention of foodborne illnesses, maintains the quality and integrity of preserved foods, and upholds the trust and well-being of those who consume them.

NECESSARY TOOLS AND EQUIPMENT FOR HOME CANNING

Here's a list of essential tools and equipment needed for home canning:

1. Canning Jars:

Mason Jars: Available in various sizes (pint, quart, half-pint), these are the most commonly used jars for canning. They have a two-piece lid system consisting of a flat metal lid and a screw band.

Specialized Canning Jars: Some specialty jars, like jelly jars, wide-mouth jars, or jars specifically designed for certain preservation methods, might be used depending on the recipe and purpose.

2. Two-Piece Lids:

Flat Metal Lids: These have a sealing compound and are used once for sealing jars. They should not be reused for canning.

Screw Bands/Rings: The metal bands hold the lids in place during processing but are not used for creating the seal. They can be reused unless they get damaged or rusted.

3. Canning Equipment:

Water Bath Canner: A large pot with a fitted lid and a rack inside. It is used for water bath canning high-acid foods like fruits, pickles, and jams.

Pressure Canner: Essential for canning low-acid foods like vegetables, meats, and soups. It uses pressure to reach higher temperatures for safe canning.

4. Utensils:

Jar Lifter: Allows you to safely lift hot jars in and out of canners without touching them with your hands.

Canning Funnel: A wide-mouthed funnel that helps in filling jars cleanly and without spills.

Lid Wand/Magnetic Lid Lifter: A tool with a magnet at the end to lift hot lids out of hot water without touching them.

Bubble Remover/Debubbler: Used to release trapped air bubbles in filled jars to ensure proper sealing.

5. Thermometer:

Candy/Preserving Thermometer: Essential for monitoring temperatures during certain canning processes, especially in sugar syrup or jelly-making.

6. Other Miscellaneous Items:

• Clean Dish Towels or Paper Towels: Used for cleaning jar rims and spills during canning.

• Cutting Boards, Knives, and Peeler: For preparing fruits and vegetables before canning.

• Timer: Important for timing processing intervals accurately.

• Labels and Permanent Marker: For labeling jars with content and date.

• Pot Holders or Heat-Resistant Gloves: Essential for handling hot jars and equipment.

• Salt and Vinegar: Common ingredients used in many preserving recipes.

• Quality Ingredients: Ensure you're using fresh, high-quality produce for the best results.

Remember, while these tools are essential, always refer to specific canning recipes and guidelines for any additional or specialized equipment needed for particular preservation methods. Following instructions meticulously is crucial for safe and successful home canning.

TIPS ON SELECTING AND MAINTAINING HOME CANNING EQUIPMENT.

Selecting and maintaining home canning equipment is vital for safe and effective preservation. Here are some tips to help you choose and upkeep your canning gear:

Selecting Home Canning Equipment:

• Quality Over Price: Invest in high-quality, purpose-built canning equipment rather than opting for cheaper alternatives. Quality equipment ensures better results and longevity.

• Match Equipment to Your Needs: Consider the types of foods you'll be canning and choose equipment accordingly. Ensure your canner (water bath or pressure canner) matches the acidity levels of the foods you plan to preserve.

• Check for Compatibility: Ensure jars, lids, and bands are compatible with each other and are specifically designed for home canning to ensure proper sealing and safety.

• Research Brands and Reviews: Look for reputable brands known for producing durable and reliable canning equipment. Reading reviews and seeking recommendations can help in making informed choices.

• Consider Durability and Ease of Cleaning: Choose equipment that is durable and easy to clean to ensure it remains in good condition for a long time.

Maintaining Home Canning Equipment:

• Inspect Equipment Regularly: Before each use, inspect jars, lids, bands, and canners for any signs of damage, rust, or wear. Damaged equipment can compromise the canning process.

• Follow Manufacturer's Instructions: Always adhere to the manufacturer's instructions for cleaning and maintaining your canning equipment. Clean equipment after each use according to recommended guidelines.

• Proper Storage: Store your canning equipment in a clean and dry environment to prevent rust or damage. Ensure they are stored in a way that avoids impacts that could cause breakage.

• Replace Damaged Parts: Replace worn-out or damaged parts, such as lids with bent edges or bands that show signs of rust. Using compromised equipment can lead to seal failures.

• Calibration and Testing: Periodically check the accuracy of thermometers or gauges on your canners to ensure proper temperature control. This is crucial, especially for pressure canners.

• Oil Moving Parts (if applicable): For pressure canners with moving parts, follow manufacturer recommendations for oiling these parts to ensure smooth functioning.

• Educate Yourself on Maintenance: Familiarize yourself with specific maintenance tips provided by the manufacturer for each piece of equipment you use.

• Keep Manuals and Guidelines Handy: Store equipment manuals and guidelines in an easily accessible place for reference and troubleshooting.

By carefully selecting quality equipment suited to your needs and maintaining it properly, you ensure the safety, effectiveness, and longevity of your home canning gear, which is crucial for successful food preservation. Always prioritize safety measures and follow recommended guidelines for proper use and maintenance of canning equipment.

THE TYPES OF CANNING

There are various types of canning methods, each suited for preserving different types of food based on their acidity levels. The two primary methods of canning are Water Bath Canning and Pressure Canning.

1. Water Bath Canning:

Suitable for: High-acid foods such as fruits, pickles, jams, jellies, and some tomatoes (acidic varieties).

Process:

• Preparation: Food is prepared, packed into jars, and sealed with lids and bands.

• Boiling Water Bath: Jars are submerged in a large pot of boiling water, ensuring the water level covers the jars by 1-2 inches.

• Processing: The jars are boiled for a specific time according to the recipe and adjusted for altitude.

• Purpose: The high acidity in these foods prevents the growth of harmful bacteria and makes them safe to process in a water bath, which heats the contents to 212°F (100°C).

2. Pressure Canning:

Suitable for: Low-acid foods such as vegetables, meats, poultry, seafood, and soups.

Process:

• Preparation: Food is prepared, packed into jars, and sealed with lids and bands.

• Pressure Canner: The jars are placed in a specialized pressure canner that seals tightly to create a high-pressure environment.

• Processing: The canner heats the contents to temperatures above 240°F (116°C) at a specific pressure according to the recipe and adjusted for altitude.

• Purpose: Low-acid foods require higher temperatures to kill harmful bacteria, molds, and spores, including Clostridium botulinum. Pressure canning achieves these higher temperatures needed for safe preservation.

Other Methods of Canning:

• Open Kettle Canning: Not recommended due to safety concerns. Food is filled into jars and sealed without further processing, which poses a higher risk of bacterial contamination and spoilage.

• Steam Canning: Similar to water bath canning, but uses steam instead of boiling water. While some sources consider it safe for high-acid foods, others advise against it due to uncertain temperature control and safety concerns.

• Oven Canning: Not recommended due to uneven heat distribution and inability to reach the high temperatures required for safe canning. It poses risks of food spoilage and bacterial growth.

Considerations for Safe Canning:

• Always use reliable, tested, and approved canning recipes from trusted sources like the USDA or the National Center for Home Food Preservation.

• Follow precise instructions for processing times, jar sizes, headspace, and altitude adjustments.

• Regularly inspect and maintain canning equipment for safe and effective use.

Choosing the appropriate canning method based on the acidity of the food being preserved is crucial for ensuring the safety and quality of home-canned goods.

THE TYPES OF FOODS SUITABLE FOR HOME CANNING AND THEIR SPECIFIC REqUIREMENTS.

Home canning is suitable for a variety of foods, but the method and specific requirements can vary based on the acidity of the food. The two primary methods for home canning are water bath canning and pressure canning. Here's an overview of foods suitable for each method along with their specific requirements:

Water Bath Canning:

High-Acid Foods (pH 4.6 or below):

1. Fruits:

Requirements: High-acid fruits like apples, berries, cherries, peaches, and pears can be canned using a water bath canner. They often require sugar, syrup, or fruit juice to pack.

2. Fruit Juices and Jams:

Requirements: Fruit juices, jams, jellies, and fruit preserves are high in acidity and suitable for water bath canning. Additional sugar and pectin may be added for gelling.

3. Pickles:

Requirements: Pickles made with vinegar (usually 5% acidity) and high-acid vegetables like cucumbers can be safely water bath canned. Follow approved recipes for pickling.

Pressure Canning:

Low-Acid Foods (pH above 4.6):

1. Vegetables:

Requirements: Low-acid vegetables like beans, peas, corn, carrots, and mixed vegetables require pressure canning due to their low acidity. The high heat of pressure canning is necessary to kill harmful bacteria like Clostridium botulinum.

2. Meats and Poultry:

Requirements: All types of meats, including beef, pork, chicken, and fish, are low in acidity and must be pressure canned for safety. Follow recommended processing times and pressure levels.

3. Soups, Stews, and Broths:

Requirements: Soups, stews, and broths made with low-acid ingredients need pressure canning. Follow guidelines for safe canning of liquid foods with meat and vegetables.

General Canning Requirements:

• Cleanliness: Ensure all equipment, jars, and utensils are thoroughly cleaned and sterilized before use.

• Quality Ingredients: Use fresh, high-quality ingredients. Avoid overripe or spoiled produce.

• Approved Recipes: Follow scientifically tested and approved canning recipes from reputable sources to ensure safe acidity levels, processing times, and pressure levels.

• Proper Processing Times and Altitude Adjustments: Adjust processing times according to altitude and follow recommended procedures for both water bath and pressure canning.

• Jar Preparation: Use appropriate jar sizes, leaving recommended headspace. Properly seal jars with new lids and bands, following the manufacturer's instructions.

By understanding the acidity levels of foods and following the specific requirements for water bath or pressure canning, you can safely preserve a wide range of fruits, vegetables, meats, and other foods for long-term storage. Always prioritize safety and follow approved guidelines to prevent foodborne illnesses.

CHAPTER TWO

STEP-BY-STEP INSTRUCTIONS FOR WATER BATH CANNING

Here's a detailed step-by-step guide for water bath canning:

Equipment:

• Water bath canner with a fitted lid and rack.

• Canning jars, lids, and bands in good condition.

• Canning funnel, jar lifter, lid wand, bubble remover.

• Clean towels, cutting board, knives, and utensils.

Instructions:

1. Wash jars, lids, and bands in hot, soapy water. Rinse thoroughly.

2. Sterilize jars by boiling them in water for 10 minutes or run them through a dishwasher's sterilization cycle.

3. Keep jars hot until ready for filling (place them in simmering water or the oven at a low temperature).

4. Wash, peel, core, slice, or chop fruits or vegetables according to the recipe.

5. Prepare any syrups, brines, or sauces needed for the canning recipe.

6. Using a canning funnel, fill the hot, sterilized jars with prepared food, leaving the recommended headspace specified in the recipe (usually around ¼ to ½ inch).

7. Remove air bubbles by running a non-metallic spatula or bubble remover along the inside of the jar.

8. Wipe the jar rims with a clean, damp cloth to ensure a clean seal.

9. Place a flat metal lid on each jar and screw on the band until fingertip-tight (not too tight).

10. Using a jar lifter, carefully place the filled and sealed jars onto the rack in the canner, ensuring they don't touch each other.

11. Fill the canner with enough hot water to cover the jars by at least 1-2 inches. Put the lid on the canner and bring the water to a rolling boil.

12. Once the water reaches a full rolling boil, start the processing time as specified in the recipe. Keep the water boiling throughout the entire processing time.

13. After processing, turn off the heat and carefully remove the jars using a jar lifter.

14. Place the jars on a towel or cooling rack, leaving space between them, to cool completely. Avoid moving or jostling them.

15. After cooling, check the seals by pressing down on the center of the lids. Properly sealed lids should not flex or pop.

16. Label the sealed jars with the contents and date before storing them in a cool, dark place away from direct sunlight.

Additional Tips:

• Always use tested and approved recipes from reliable sources like the USDA or the National Center for Home Food Preservation.

• Adjust processing times for altitude if necessary.

• Avoid over-tightening jar bands as this can prevent proper air escape during processing.

• Use caution when working with hot jars and equipment to prevent burns.

STEP-BY-STEP INSTRUCTIONS FOR PRESSURE CANNING

Here's a comprehensive step-by-step guide for pressure canning:

Equipment:

• Pressure canner in good working condition with a fitted lid, pressure gauge, and sealing gasket.

• Canning jars, lids, and bands in good condition.

• Canning funnel, jar lifter, lid wand, bubble remover.

• Clean towels, cutting board, knives, and utensils.

Instructions:

1. Check the pressure canner for any damage or defects, ensuring the sealing gasket is in good condition. Check the pressure gauge for accuracy.

2. Wash jars, lids, and bands in hot, soapy water. Rinse thoroughly.

3. Sterilize jars by boiling them in water for 10 minutes or run them through a dishwasher's sterilization cycle.

4. Keep jars hot until ready for filling (place them in simmering water or the oven at a low temperature).

5. Wash and prepare the low-acid food you intend to can according to the recipe. Follow the recipe guidelines for any pre-cooking or seasoning requirements.

6. Using a canning funnel, fill the hot, sterilized jars with prepared food, leaving the recommended headspace specified in the recipe (typically 1 to 1.5 inches).

7. Remove air bubbles by running a non-metallic spatula or bubble remover along the inside of the jar.

8. Wipe the jar rims with a clean, damp cloth to ensure a clean seal.

9. Place a flat metal lid on each jar and screw on the band until fingertip-tight (not too tight).

10. Add the required amount of water to the pressure canner as specified in the manufacturer's instructions.

11. Place the filled and sealed jars on the canner's rack, ensuring they don't touch each other.

12. Securely fasten the lid onto the pressure canner and ensure the vent pipe is clear.

13. Heat the canner with the lid locked but without the pressure regulator in place to allow steam to escape for about 10 minutes.

14. Place the pressure regulator or weight on the vent pipe to build pressure according to the recipe and your altitude adjustments.

15. Follow the canner's instructions to reach and maintain the recommended pressure.

16. Once the canner reaches the required pressure, start the processing time as specified in the recipe.

17. Maintain the recommended pressure throughout the entire processing time.

18. After processing, turn off the heat and let the pressure drop naturally. Avoid forcing the pressure to drop by cooling the canner or lifting the weight.

19. Once the pressure has dropped to zero and it's safe to open, carefully remove the jars using a jar lifter.

20. Place the jars on a towel or cooling rack, leaving space between them, to cool completely.

21. Check the seals after cooling; properly sealed lids should not flex or pop.

22. Label the sealed jars with the contents and date before storing them in a cool, dark place away from direct sunlight.

Additional Tips:

• Always use tested and approved recipes from reliable sources like the USDA or the National Center for Home Food Preservation.

• Adjust processing times for altitude if necessary.

• Avoid over-tightening jar bands as this can prevent proper air escape during processing.

• Use caution when working with hot jars and equipment to prevent burns.

THE VARIOUS PRESERVING TECHNIqUES

Preserving techniques are diverse methods used to extend the shelf life of food, maintain its quality, and prevent spoilage. These methods vary based on the type of food, desired flavor, texture, and storage preferences. Here are various preserving techniques in detail:

1. Canning:

Water Bath Canning: Ideal for high-acid foods like fruits, pickles, jams, and jellies. The process involves submerging filled jars in boiling water to create a vacuum seal that prevents bacterial growth.

Pressure Canning: Suitable for low-acid foods like vegetables, meats, and soups. This method involves using a pressure canner to reach high temperatures above boiling, necessary for safe preservation.

2. Pickling:

Vinegar Pickling: Involves submerging vegetables or fruits in a vinegar solution, often with added spices or herbs. The acidity of vinegar inhibits bacterial growth and adds a tangy flavor to the food.

Fermented Pickling: Utilizes the process of fermentation using saltwater brine or lacto-fermentation to create an environment where beneficial bacteria naturally preserve the food. Examples include sauerkraut, kimchi, or traditional pickles.

3. Jams, Jellies, and Preserves:

Jam Making: Involves cooking crushed or chopped fruits with sugar and pectin to create a thick, spreadable consistency.

Jelly Making: Similar to jam but involves straining fruit juice to remove solids, resulting in a clear, firm spread.

Preserves: Whole or large pieces of fruit preserved in a sugar syrup. They retain their shape and texture better than jams or jellies.

4. Dehydration:

Air Drying: Involves laying thin slices of fruits, vegetables, or herbs in a single layer and allowing them to air dry naturally, preserving them by removing moisture.

Oven Drying: Similar to air drying but uses an oven set to low temperatures to speed up the drying process.

Dehydrator: Uses specialized equipment with controlled temperatures and airflow to efficiently dry foods while preserving their flavors and nutrients.

5. Freezing:

Simple Freezing: Involves placing prepared food items in suitable freezer containers or bags and freezing them at 0°F (-18°C) or below. It's a quick and easy preservation method but may affect texture.

Blanching: Pre-treating vegetables by briefly immersing them in boiling water before freezing. This helps retain color, texture, and nutrients.

6. Smoking and Curing:

Smoking: Preserving food by exposing it to smoke from burning wood or other materials. Commonly used for meats, fish, and cheese to add flavor and aid preservation.

Curing: Preserving food by using salt, sugar, or nitrites to draw out moisture, inhibit bacterial growth, and enhance flavor. Commonly used for meats, particularly in making bacon or ham.

7. Oil and Vinegar Infusion:

Herb-infused Oils: Preserving herbs in oil to create flavorful infusions used in cooking or as condiments.

Fruit or Herb Vinegars: Infusing vinegar with fruits, herbs, or spices to create flavored vinegars used in dressings, marinades, or as a culinary ingredient.

Considerations for Safe Preserving:

- Use fresh, high-quality ingredients.

- Follow approved and tested recipes from reliable sources.

• Properly sterilize equipment and containers.

• Maintain hygiene and cleanliness throughout the preserving process.

Each preserving technique offers unique flavors, textures, and advantages, allowing individuals to enjoy seasonal produce year-round while adding variety to their meals. It's essential to choose the right method based on the type of food, personal preferences, and desired storage duration.

RECIPES FOR EACH TECHNIqUE LISTED ABOVE

Water Bath Canning Recipe (Tomato Sauce)

Ingredients:

• 15 lbs ripe tomatoes

• 2 cups chopped onions

• 4 cloves garlic, minced

• 2 tsp salt

• 2 tbsp olive oil

• 1/4 cup fresh basil leaves

• Lemon juice (for acidity)

Equipment:

- Large stockpot

- Water bath canner with rack

- Canning jars, lids, and bands

- Canning funnel

- Jar lifter

- Ladle

- Non-metallic spatula or bubble remover

Instructions:

1. Wash tomatoes thoroughly and score an "X" on the bottom of each. Blanch tomatoes in boiling water for 1-2 minutes, then transfer to an ice bath.

2. Peel off the skins, core, and remove seeds. Coarsely chop the tomatoes.

3. In a large pot, sauté chopped onions and minced garlic in olive oil until softened.

4. Add chopped tomatoes and basil leaves. Simmer uncovered, stirring occasionally, for 1-2 hours until the sauce thickens.

5. While the sauce simmers, prepare the jars and adjust acidity. Add lemon juice to each jar: 2 tablespoons per quart jar or 1 tablespoon per pint jar.

6. Wash jars, lids, and bands in hot, soapy water. Rinse thoroughly.

7. Sterilize jars by boiling them in a water bath canner or using a dishwasher's sterilization cycle. Keep them hot until ready for filling.

8. Fill the water bath canner with enough water to cover jars by 1-2 inches. Bring it to a simmer.

9. Using a canning funnel, fill hot, sterilized jars with the hot tomato sauce, leaving 1/2-inch headspace.

10. Slide a non-metallic spatula or bubble remover around the inside of the jar to release air bubbles. Wipe the jar rims with a clean, damp cloth to ensure a clean seal.

11. Place a flat metal lid on each jar and screw on the band until fingertip-tight (not too tight).

12. Using a jar lifter, carefully place the filled and sealed jars onto the rack in the canner, ensuring they don't touch each other.

13. Lower the rack into the simmering water. Ensure the water covers the jars by 1-2 inches.

14. Cover the canner and bring the water to a rolling boil. Process jars for 35-40 minutes (adjusting for altitude) for quarts or pints.

15. After processing, turn off the heat and carefully remove jars using a jar lifter.

16. Place jars on a towel or cooling rack, leaving space between them, and let them cool completely.

17. Check for seals (lids should not flex when pressed), label with contents and date, and store in a cool, dark place.

Fermented Pickles Recipe

Ingredients:

• 3-4 lbs pickling cucumbers

• 4 cups water

• 2 tbsp pickling salt

• 2-3 cloves garlic, peeled

• Fresh dill

• Spices (optional: mustard seeds, coriander seeds, peppercorns)

Equipment:

• Large glass or ceramic container (crock or jar)

• Weight or smaller jar to keep cucumbers submerged

• Clean cloth or cheesecloth

• Rubber band or string

Instructions:

1. Wash Cucumbers: Rinse cucumbers thoroughly under running water. Trim off any blossom ends.

2. In a large non-metallic container, dissolve pickling salt in water to create a brine solution. Allow it to cool to room temperature.

3. Wash the fermenting container (crock or jar) with hot, soapy water. Rinse thoroughly.

4. Sterilize by pouring boiling water into the container and allowing it to sit for a few minutes. Discard the water.

5. Place peeled garlic cloves, fresh dill, and any optional spices into the bottom of the sterilized container.

6. Pack the prepared cucumbers vertically into the container over the aromatics, ensuring they fit snugly.

7. Pour the cooled brine over the cucumbers, making sure they are completely submerged. Leave about 2 inches of headspace.

8. Place a clean weight or smaller jar inside the container to keep the cucumbers submerged under the brine. This prevents exposure to air.

9. Cover the container with a clean cloth or cheesecloth secured with a rubber band or string. This allows air to flow while keeping out debris.

10. Store the container in a cool, dark place away from direct sunlight (ideally around 65-75°F or 18-24°C).

11. Check daily to ensure cucumbers remain submerged. Skim off any scum that forms on the surface.

12. Fermentation time can vary (approximately 3-7 days) depending on room temperature and desired sourness. Taste occasionally for preferred tanginess.

13. Cucumbers are ready when they reach the desired level of sourness. They should have a pleasant tangy taste.

14. Remove weight and aromatics. Pack fermented pickles into clean, sterilized jars, leaving headspace.

15. Seal jars and store fermented pickles in the refrigerator. They will continue to ferment, albeit at a slower rate, in cold storage.

Dehydrating Fruits

Ingredients:

• Fresh fruits (apples, bananas, berries, mangoes, etc.)

• Dehydrator or oven

• Lemon juice (optional, for preventing browning)

Instructions:

1. Wash the fruits thoroughly under running water.

2. Peel, core, and slice the fruits evenly into consistent sizes (about ¼ to ½ inch thick). Remove seeds and pits as needed.

3. Optional Pre-Treatment: Some fruits prone to browning (like apples) can be briefly soaked in a solution of water and lemon juice (1 tablespoon per quart of water) to preserve color.

4. Arrange the prepared fruit slices in a single layer on the dehydrator trays, ensuring they don't touch or overlap.

5. Follow the dehydrator manufacturer's instructions for temperature and settings. Typically, fruits are dehydrated at 125-135°F (52-57°C) for several hours to overnight.

6. Rotate trays occasionally for even drying.

7. Oven Method: If using an oven, place the fruit slices on baking sheets lined with parchment paper or silicone mats.

8. Set the oven temperature to the lowest setting (usually around 140-150°F or 60-65°C).

9. Prop the oven door open slightly with a wooden spoon or oven-safe object to allow moisture to escape.

10. Check and rotate the trays regularly for even drying.

11. Fruits are adequately dehydrated when they are leathery, pliable, and no longer moist but not overly dry or brittle. Larger or juicier fruits might take longer (12-24 hours) to dehydrate fully.

12. Once dried, allow the fruits to cool to room temperature on the trays or baking sheets.

13. Conditioning (Optional): For even moisture distribution, conditioning is recommended. Place the cooled dried fruits in airtight containers or zipper-lock bags, filling them halfway. Seal and store in a cool, dry place for a few days, shaking occasionally.

14. After conditioning, pack the completely cooled and dried fruits into airtight containers, zipper-lock bags, or vacuum-sealed bags.

15. Label the containers with the fruit type and date of dehydration.

16. Store the dehydrated fruits in a cool, dark place away from moisture and sunlight to maintain quality. The pantry or a cupboard is suitable for short-term storage, or use the refrigerator or freezer for longer shelf life.

Tips:

• Different fruits have varying dehydration times; thicker slices or juicier fruits take longer to dry.

• Properly dried fruits should feel leathery with no moisture when touched.

• Over-dried fruits become brittle and lose flavor and nutritional value.

• Store dehydrated fruits in airtight containers to maintain freshness.

Simple Freezing (Berries)

Ingredients:

- Fresh berries (strawberries, blueberries, raspberries, etc.)

- Baking sheet or tray

- Parchment paper or silicone mat

- Freezer-safe bags or containers

Instructions:

1. Wash the berries gently under cold running water to remove any dirt or debris.

2. Pat them dry with a clean kitchen towel or paper towels. Ensure they are completely dry to prevent freezer burn.

3. Remove stems, leaves, and any spoiled or damaged berries.

4. Line a baking sheet or tray with parchment paper or a silicone mat. This will prevent the berries from sticking to the surface.

5. Spread the prepared berries in a single layer on the lined baking sheet or tray, ensuring they are not touching or overlapping.

6. For larger berries like strawberries, you might want to halve or slice them to freeze more evenly.

7. Place the baking sheet or tray in the freezer and allow the berries to pre-freeze for about 1-2 hours or until they are firm but not completely frozen.

8. Once the berries are pre-frozen, quickly transfer them into freezer-safe bags or containers.

9. Remove excess air from the bags as much as possible before sealing to prevent freezer burn. Consider using a straw to remove air if using zip-top bags.

10. Label the freezer bags or containers with the type of berries and the date of freezing for easy identification.

11. Store the bags or containers of berries in the freezer at 0°F (-18°C) or below for optimal preservation.

Tips:

• Pre-freezing berries on a tray before packaging prevents them from clumping together in the bags, making it easier to grab small portions.

• Use frozen berries within 6-12 months for best quality.

• Berries can be used directly from the freezer in smoothies, baked goods, jams, or thawed for toppings or snacking.

Smoking Salmon

Ingredients:

- Fresh salmon fillets (skin-on or skinless)

- Kosher salt

- Brown sugar

- Black pepper

- Wood chips (hickory, applewood, alder, etc.)

- Smoker (electric, charcoal, or gas)

- Smoker thermometer

- Aluminum foil or drip pan

Instructions:

1. Rinse the salmon fillets under cold water and pat them dry with paper towels. If necessary, remove any remaining pin bones using tweezers.

2. In a bowl, mix together a brine solution using kosher salt, brown sugar, and black pepper. Use a ratio of approximately 1:1 salt to sugar.

3. Generously coat the salmon fillets with the brine mixture, ensuring both sides are covered.

4. Place the fillets in a shallow dish or a large resealable plastic bag and refrigerate. Brine for about 6-12 hours, depending on the thickness of the fillets.

5. Soak the wood chips in water for at least 30 minutes before smoking. This helps generate smoke and prolongs their burning time.

6. Follow the manufacturer's instructions for your specific smoker type.

7. Preheat the smoker to a low temperature, ideally around 180°F (82°C). Ensure proper ventilation for smoke to escape.

8. Line the smoker tray or a drip pan with aluminum foil for easy cleanup. You can also place a drip pan filled with water below the salmon to help maintain moisture.

9. Remove the salmon fillets from the brine and rinse them thoroughly under cold water to remove excess salt. Pat them dry with paper towels.

10. Place the salmon fillets on a cooling rack or tray and let them air-dry for 1-2 hours until a sticky surface called a pellicle forms. This step helps the smoke adhere to the fish.

11. Place the salmon fillets directly on the smoker racks, leaving space between them for air circulation.

12. Add the soaked wood chips to the smoker box or directly to the coals to generate smoke.

13. Smoke the salmon at the preheated temperature for approximately 1.5 to 3 hours, depending on fillet thickness, until it reaches an internal temperature of 145°F (63°C).

14. Monitor the smoker temperature using a smoker thermometer, adjusting vents or adding more wood chips to maintain a consistent low heat.

15. Once smoked, carefully remove the salmon from the smoker and let it cool on a wire rack. Allow the smoked salmon to rest for about 30 minutes before refrigerating.

16. Refrigerate the smoked salmon in airtight containers or zipper-lock bags for short-term storage (up to a week) or freeze for longer shelf life (up to several months).

17. Enjoy your homemade smoked salmon as a flavorful appetizer, in salads, pasta dishes, or sandwiches. Adjust smoking times and flavors according to personal preferences. Ensure thorough cooking and safe internal temperatures for the salmon.

Herb-Infused Oil

Ingredients:

• Fresh herbs (basil, rosemary, thyme, etc.)

• Good-quality oil (olive oil, vegetable oil)

• Sterilized glass jars or bottles with lids

• Fine-mesh sieve or cheesecloth

• Funnel

• Small saucepan

Instructions:

1. Rinse the fresh herbs under running water and gently pat them dry with paper towels. Ensure they are completely dry to prevent microbial growth.

2. Wash glass jars or bottles and lids in hot, soapy water. Rinse thoroughly.

3. Sterilize them by boiling in water for 10 minutes or using a dishwasher's sterilization cycle.

4. Pour the desired amount of oil into a clean saucepan. Warm the oil over low heat; do not bring it to a boil.

5. Bruise or slightly crush the herbs to release their flavors. This can be done by gently rolling them between your hands or using a mortar and pestle.

6. Once the oil is warm (not hot), add the prepared herbs to the saucepan.

7. Simmer the herbs in the oil over low heat for 5-10 minutes to infuse the flavors. Avoid overheating or boiling the oil.

8. Remove the saucepan from heat and let the infused oil cool to room temperature.

9. Strain the oil through a fine-mesh sieve or cheesecloth into a clean bowl or directly into sterilized jars, removing the herbs. A funnel can help with pouring.

10. Pour the strained infused oil into sterilized glass jars or bottles, leaving a little space at the top. Seal tightly with lids.

11. Store the herb-infused oil in a cool, dark place away from direct sunlight or heat sources.

12. Use the oil within a week or two for optimal flavor and safety. Refrigeration can extend the shelf life slightly, but it's best to use it within a short period.

13. Infused oils should be refrigerated and used within a short time to reduce the risk of bacterial growth and botulism.

14. Discard any infused oil that shows signs of spoilage, cloudiness, or an off odor.

15. If making larger batches for long-term storage, consider adding a small amount of citric acid or using commercial preservatives to increase safety.

SAFETY MEASURES, INCLUDING PROPER CLEANING, STERILIZATION, AND JAR SEALING TECHNIqUES.

Safety measures in preserving food are crucial to prevent contamination, spoilage, and foodborne illnesses. Here are detailed guidelines for cleaning, sterilization, and jar sealing techniques:

Cleaning and Sterilization:

• Clean Working Surfaces: Ensure your countertops, utensils, and equipment are clean before starting the preserving process. Wash with hot, soapy water and rinse thoroughly.

• Wash Hands Thoroughly: Wash hands frequently with soap and warm water for at least 20 seconds before handling food, jars, or utensils.

• Clean Produce: Wash fruits and vegetables thoroughly under running water before preserving them.

Sterilize Jars, Lids, and Bands:

• Wash jars, lids, and bands in hot, soapy water. Rinse them well.

• Sterilize jars by boiling them in a water bath canner or using the dishwasher's sterilization cycle.

• Keep jars hot until ready for filling, either by keeping them in simmering water or in a low-temperature oven.

• Sterilize Equipment: Ensure all utensils, canning tools, funnels, and ladles are clean and sanitized before use.

Jar Sealing Techniques:

• Proper Filling: Fill jars with the prepared food, leaving the recommended headspace specified in the recipe. Headspace allows for proper expansion during processing and ensures a good seal.

• Removing Air Bubbles: Use a bubble remover or a non-metallic spatula to release trapped air bubbles by sliding it along the inside of the jar.

• Wiping Jar Rims: After filling, wipe the rims of the jars with a clean, damp cloth to remove any food particles, ensuring a clean seal.

Applying Lids and Bands:

• Place flat metal lids on the jars using a lid wand or magnetic lid lifter.

• Screw on the bands until they are fingertip-tight. Do not over-tighten, as this can prevent air from escaping during processing.

Sealing Techniques for Canning:

Water Bath Canning:

• Ensure the water level in the canner covers the jars by 1-2 inches.

• Process jars in the boiling water for the specified time according to the recipe.

Pressure Canning:

• Seal the pressure canner tightly and allow steam to vent for 10 minutes before sealing.

• Process jars at the correct pressure according to the recipe and maintain this pressure for the specified time.

General Safety Tips:

• Use only tested and approved recipes from reliable sources.

• Adjust processing times for altitude as necessary.

• Inspect jars, lids, and bands for damage before use. Discard any damaged components.

• Label jars with contents and date to track freshness and storage time.

By adhering to proper cleaning, sterilization, and sealing techniques, you can ensure the safety and success of your home-preserving endeavors, reducing the risk of contamination and ensuring longer-lasting, high-quality preserved foods.

COMMON MISTAKES WHEN CANNING AND HOW TO AVOID THEM

Canning is a wonderful way to preserve food, but it's essential to avoid common mistakes to ensure safety and successful preservation. Here are some common mistakes when canning and how to prevent them:

1. Not Following Approved Recipes or Procedures:

Mistake: Using untested recipes or altering ingredient proportions in canning recipes.

Prevention: Use only scientifically tested and approved canning recipes from reputable sources like USDA, Ball, or other reliable canning guides. Follow recipes precisely to ensure proper acidity, processing times, and ratios.

2. Inadequate Sterilization and Cleaning:

Mistake: Improperly cleaning jars or equipment, leading to contamination.

Prevention: Wash jars, lids, and equipment in hot, soapy water and sterilize them before use. Use a water bath or dishwasher's sterilization cycle for jars and boil or sanitize utensils.

3. Insufficient Processing Time or Temperature:

Mistake: Not processing jars for the required time or temperature, leading to under-processed food and potential spoilage.

Prevention: Use a reliable and accurate timer or thermometer. Follow the recommended processing times and temperatures specified in approved canning recipes for your altitude.

4. Overfilling or Underfilling Jars:

Mistake: Filling jars improperly, either too full or not leaving enough headspace.

Prevention: Leave the recommended headspace (specified in recipes) to allow for expansion during processing. Use a canning funnel for accurate filling.

5. Ignoring Altitude Adjustments:

Mistake: Not adjusting canning times for altitude, affecting the safety of preserved foods.

Prevention: Refer to altitude adjustments for canning times provided in reliable canning guides or recipes. Water boils at lower temperatures at higher altitudes, requiring longer processing times.

6. Reusing Lids or Using Damaged Equipment:

Mistake: Reusing canning lids or using damaged lids, leading to improper sealing.

Prevention: Use new lids for each canning session. Inspect jars, lids, and bands for dents, rust, or damage. Discard any damaged components.

7. Not Checking Seals and Storing Improperly:

Mistake: Not checking jar seals or storing jars in unsuitable conditions.

Prevention: After processing, check for sealed lids (lids should not flex when pressed). Store properly in a cool, dark place. Label jars with contents and date for easy identification.

8. Using Non-Acidic Foods in Water Bath Canning:

Mistake: Water bath canning non-acidic foods (e.g., vegetables, meats) that require pressure canning for safety.

Prevention: Use a pressure canner for low-acid foods to eliminate the risk of bacterial contamination. Follow recommended methods for different food types.

By being mindful of these common mistakes and following safe canning practices outlined in approved recipes and guides, you can ensure safe, successful, and flavorful home-canned foods.

PROPER STORAGE CONDITIONS FOR CANNED FOODS.

Proper storage conditions for canned foods are crucial to maintain their quality, safety, and shelf life. Here are guidelines for storing home-canned foods:

1. Check Seals and Labels:

Check Seals: After canning, ensure the jars have properly sealed. A sealed lid should not flex or pop when pressed. Any unsealed jars should be refrigerated and used promptly.

Labeling: Label jars with the contents and date of canning. This helps you track freshness and identify contents easily.

2. Store in a Cool, Dark Place:

Temperature: Store canned foods in a cool, dry, and consistently cool location. Ideally, aim for temperatures between 50-70°F (10-21°C). Avoid areas prone to temperature fluctuations, such as near stoves, ovens, or in direct sunlight.

Darkness: Keep canned goods away from direct light, as light can degrade colors, flavors, and nutrients in the food.

3. Use FIFO (First In, First Out):

Rotation: Practice FIFO to ensure older canned goods are used first. Place newly canned items behind older ones on shelves to promote using older stock before it reaches its expiration.

4. Avoid Extreme Conditions:

Humidity: Prevent excessive moisture. Avoid storing canned goods in areas prone to high humidity or dampness, as it can cause rusting of lids or compromise the seals.

Freezing: While canned goods are safe from bacterial contamination, freezing temperatures might cause the lids to loosen or crack. Avoid freezing canned foods unless explicitly instructed in a recipe (e.g., fruit-based jams for extended storage).

5. Monitor and Inspect:

Check Periodically: Periodically inspect canned goods for signs of spoilage. Look for bulging lids, leaking jars, off odors, or any other unusual changes. Discard any cans showing signs of spoilage or damage.

Storage Duration: While properly canned foods can last for a year or longer, it's best to consume them within a year for optimal quality. High-acid foods like fruits and pickles can often last longer than low-acid foods like meats and vegetables.

6. Refrigerate Opened Jars:

Opened Jars: Once a canned jar is opened, refrigerate any leftover contents promptly. Consume within a few days, adhering to general food safety guidelines.

7. Store Diverse Foods Separately:

Odor Transfer: Avoid storing strongly scented foods next to mild-flavored foods. Strong odors might transfer between containers, affecting the taste of the preserved food.

By adhering to these storage practices, you can maximize the shelf life and quality of your home-canned foods while ensuring they remain safe for consumption. Always err on the side of caution and discard any canned food showing signs of spoilage or damage.

THE IMPORTANCE OF LABELING WITH DATE AND CONTENTS.

Labeling home-canned goods with both the date and contents is a critical practice that holds immense importance for several reasons:

1. Ensures Food Safety:

Identification: Labels help identify the contents of the jars, ensuring you know what's inside without needing to open them.

Allergies and Dietary Restrictions: Knowing the contents allows individuals to identify potential allergens or ingredients that may not align with their dietary restrictions.

2. Maintains Freshness and Quality:

Rotation: Date labeling enables the use of the FIFO (First In, First Out) method, ensuring older canned goods are used first, maintaining their freshness and quality.

Shelf Life Awareness: By labeling with the date of canning, you can keep track of how long the food has been in storage and use it within recommended time frames for optimal quality.

3. Prevents Waste and Confusion:

Avoids Waste: Clear labeling reduces the chances of mistakenly keeping canned goods beyond their recommended shelf life, minimizing food waste.

Prevents Confusion: Labels prevent confusion or mix-ups, especially when dealing with multiple jars of various contents or when others in the household are accessing the preserved foods.

4. Safety and Identification:

Safety Precaution: Properly labeling jars ensures that potentially hazardous contents are identified clearly, reducing the risk of accidentally consuming spoiled or inappropriate foods.

Easy Identification: Labels make it easy to identify the contents at a glance, saving time and avoiding the need to open multiple jars to find a specific item.

5. Organizational Efficiency:

Organized Storage: Labeled jars contribute to an organized pantry, allowing easy selection and organization of foods based on preference or meal planning.

6. Sharing or Gifting:

Gifting and Sharing: Clearly labeled jars make for excellent homemade gifts. The recipient can easily identify the contents and date of canning for their reference.

7. Future Reference:

Record Keeping: Labels serve as a reference for future canning sessions. You can note any changes in recipes, preferences, or adjustments made for future improvement.

In summary, labeling with the date and contents of home-canned goods is not just a recommended practice; it is a fundamental step in ensuring food safety, maintaining quality, preventing waste, and facilitating organized and efficient storage and usage.

CHAPTER THREE

WATER BATH CANNING RECIPES

Canning Apples

Ingredients/Equipment:

• Fresh apples (variety of your choice)

• Ascorbic acid or lemon juice (for preventing browning)

• Sugar (optional for syrup)

• Water bath canner

• Canning jars, lids, and bands

• Jar lifter, canning funnel, and bubble remover

Instructions:

1. Wash and Peel: Thoroughly wash the apples under running water. Peel the apples, removing the skin with a vegetable peeler or knife.

2. Core and Slice: Remove the cores and seeds from the apples. Slice or cut them into desired shapes or sizes. You can choose to slice, quarter, or cut them into chunks.

3. Prevent Browning: To prevent browning, soak the prepared apple slices in a solution of ascorbic acid or lemon juice and water (1 teaspoon of ascorbic acid or 1/4 cup lemon juice per quart of water).

4. Make Syrup (Optional): If desired, prepare a light or medium syrup by dissolving sugar in water. This step is optional but can enhance the flavor. Use about 2 cups of sugar to 6 cups of water for a medium syrup.

5. Pack Jars: Pack the prepared apple slices into clean, sterilized canning jars, leaving about 1/2 inch of headspace at the top of the jars.

6. Add Syrup (Optional): If using syrup, pour it over the apples in the jars, maintaining the recommended headspace.

7. Remove Air Bubbles: Use a bubble remover or a non-metallic utensil to release any trapped air bubbles in the jars by running it along the inside edges of the jars.

8. Wipe Jar Rims: Ensure the jar rims are clean and dry. Wipe them with a clean, damp cloth to remove any residue or stickiness.

9. Apply Lids and Bands: Place new, properly sterilized lids on the jars and secure them with bands, tightening them until fingertip tight (not too tight).

10. Prepare Water Bath Canner: Place a rack in the bottom of the water bath canner and fill it with enough water to cover the jars by at least 1 to 2 inches.

11. Heat Water: Bring the water in the canner to a boil.

12. Process Jars: Carefully place the filled jars into the canner using a jar lifter. Ensure the water covers the jars by at least 1 inch.

13. Process Time: Process pint jars for approximately 20-25 minutes and quart jars for around 25-30 minutes, adjusting for altitude as necessary.

14. Remove Jars: Once processed, turn off the heat, and carefully remove the jars using a jar lifter. Place them on a towel or rack to cool.

15. Cool and Seal: Let the jars cool undisturbed for 12-24 hours. As they cool, you'll hear the lids popping, indicating a proper seal.

16. Check Seals: After cooling, check the jar lids for a proper seal by pressing the center of each lid. If sealed, the lid should not flex or pop.

17. Store the properly sealed jars in a cool, dark place. Use the canned apples within a year for the best quality. Enjoy your home-canned apples in various recipes throughout the year!

Canning Peaches

Ingredients/Equipment:

• Fresh peaches

• Ascorbic acid or lemon juice (for preventing browning)

• Sugar (optional for syrup)

• Water bath canner

• Canning jars, lids, and bands

• Jar lifter, canning funnel, and bubble remover

Instructions:

1. Wash and Blanch: Wash the peaches thoroughly under running water. Score a small "X" on the bottom of each peach with a knife. Blanch the peaches in boiling water for about 30-60 seconds, then immediately transfer them to an ice water bath to stop the cooking process.

2. Remove Skins: Once cooled, peel off the skins of the blanched peaches. The skins should come off easily after blanching.

3. Cut and Pit: Cut the peaches in half or slice them, removing the pits. You can also leave them halved or slice them into quarters, as preferred.

4. Prevent Browning: To prevent browning, place the prepared peach slices in a solution of ascorbic acid or lemon juice and water (1 teaspoon of ascorbic acid or 1/4 cup lemon juice per quart of water).

5. Make Syrup (Optional): If desired, prepare a light or medium syrup by dissolving sugar in water. Use about 2 cups of sugar to 6 cups of water for a medium syrup.

6. Pack Jars: Pack the prepared peach slices into clean, sterilized canning jars, leaving about 1/2 inch of headspace at the top of the jars.

7. Add Syrup (Optional): If using syrup, pour it over the peaches in the jars, maintaining the recommended headspace.

8. Remove Air Bubbles: Use a bubble remover or a non-metallic utensil to release any trapped air bubbles in the jars by running it along the inside edges of the jars.

9. Wipe Jar Rims: Ensure the jar rims are clean and dry. Wipe them with a clean, damp cloth to remove any residue or stickiness.

10. Apply Lids and Bands: Place new, properly sterilized lids on the jars and secure them with bands, tightening them until fingertip tight (not too tight).

11. Prepare Water Bath Canner: Place a rack in the bottom of the water bath canner and fill it with enough water to cover the jars by at least 1 to 2 inches.

12. Heat Water: Bring the water in the canner to a boil.

13. Process Jars: Carefully place the filled jars into the canner using a jar lifter. Ensure the water covers the jars by at least 1 inch.

14. Process Time: Process pint jars for approximately 25 minutes and quart jars for around 30 minutes, adjusting for altitude as necessary.

15. Remove Jars: Once processed, turn off the heat, and carefully remove the jars using a jar lifter. Place them on a towel or rack to cool.

16. Cool and Seal: Let the jars cool undisturbed for 12-24 hours. As they cool, you'll hear the lids popping, indicating a proper seal.

17. Check Seals: After cooling, check the jar lids for a proper seal by pressing the center of each lid. If sealed, the lid should not flex or pop.

18. Store the properly sealed jars in a cool, dark place. Use the canned peaches within a year for the best quality. Enjoy your home-canned peaches in various recipes or as a delicious snack!

Canning Fruit Juice

Ingredients/Equipment:

• Fresh fruits (such as apples, grapes, berries, etc.)

• Sugar (optional, for sweetness)

• Water bath canner

• Canning jars, lids, and bands

• Cheesecloth or jelly bag

• Large pot for cooking juice

• Jar lifter, canning funnel, and ladle

Instructions:

1. Wash and Prepare Fruit: Wash the fruits thoroughly under running water. Remove stems, pits, or any spoiled parts. Chop larger fruits into smaller pieces.

2. Place the prepared fruits in a large pot and crush or mash them to release the juice.

3. Heat the fruit over low to medium heat, stirring occasionally, until the fruits release their juices and soften.

4. Alternatively, you can use a fruit juicer or extractor to extract the juice directly from the fruits without heating.

5. Strain Juice: Strain the fruit mixture through a cheesecloth or jelly bag to separate the juice from solids, allowing the juice to drip into a clean container. This helps clarify the juice.

6. Heat Juice (Optional): Heat the extracted juice in a clean pot, bringing it to a gentle simmer but avoid boiling. Heating is optional, especially if the juice was extracted with heat initially.

7. Sweeten (Optional): If desired, add sugar to the juice for sweetness. Stir until the sugar dissolves completely.

8. Prepare Jars: Wash canning jars, lids, and bands in hot, soapy water. Sterilize them by boiling in water for 10 minutes or using a dishwasher's sterilization cycle.

9. Fill Jars: Using a canning funnel, carefully pour the hot fruit juice into the prepared jars, leaving about 1/4 inch of headspace.

10. Remove Air Bubbles: Use a bubble remover or non-metallic utensil to release any air bubbles by running it along the inside edges of the jars.

11. Wipe Jar Rims: Ensure the jar rims are clean and dry. Wipe them with a clean, damp cloth to remove any residue or stickiness.

12. Apply Lids and Bands: Place sterilized lids on the jars and secure them with bands, tightening them until fingertip tight (not too tight).

13. Prepare Water Bath Canner: Place a rack in the bottom of the water bath canner and fill it with enough water to cover the jars by at least 1 to 2 inches.

14. Heat Water: Bring the water in the canner to a boil.

15. Process Jars: Carefully place the filled jars into the canner using a jar lifter. Ensure the water covers the jars by at least 1 inch.

16. Process Time: Process the jars in the boiling water bath for approximately 5-20 minutes, adjusting processing time based on the specific fruit juice being canned and your altitude.

17. Remove Jars: Once processed, turn off the heat and carefully remove the jars using a jar lifter. Place them on a towel or rack to cool.

18. Cool and Seal: Let the jars cool undisturbed for 12-24 hours. As they cool, you'll hear the lids popping, indicating a proper seal.

19. Check Seals: After cooling, check the jar lids for a proper seal by pressing the center of each lid. If sealed, the lid should not flex or pop.

20. Store the properly sealed jars in a cool, dark place. Use the canned fruit juice within a year for the best quality. Enjoy your homemade fruit juice whenever you desire a refreshing drink!

Canning Jam

Ingredients/Equipment:

• Fresh fruits (berries, peaches, apricots, etc.)

• Granulated sugar

• Pectin (optional, for gelling)

• Water bath canner

• Canning jars, lids, and bands

• Jar lifter, canning funnel, and ladle

Instructions:

1. Wash and Prepare Fruit: Wash the fruits thoroughly under running water. Remove stems, pits, or any spoiled parts. Chop larger fruits into smaller pieces.

2. Crush or Mash Fruit: Crush or mash the prepared fruit in a pot using a potato masher or fork to release juices and create the desired consistency for the jam.

3. Cook Fruit: Place the mashed fruit in a large pot or saucepan. Cook the fruit over medium heat, stirring occasionally, until it softens and begins to simmer.

4. Add Sugar and Pectin: Gradually add sugar to the fruit, stirring continuously until the sugar dissolves. If using pectin for gelling, follow the manufacturer's instructions and add it to the mixture accordingly.

5. Boil Jam Mixture: Increase the heat to bring the fruit and sugar mixture to a rolling boil. Stir frequently to prevent sticking or burning. Continue boiling until the jam thickens, reaches the desired consistency, and passes the gel test (dropping a small amount on a chilled plate to check for thickness).

6. Prepare Jars: Wash canning jars, lids, and bands in hot, soapy water. Sterilize them by boiling in water for 10 minutes or using a dishwasher's sterilization cycle.

7. Fill Jars: Using a ladle and canning funnel, carefully fill the hot, sterilized jars with the hot jam mixture, leaving about 1/4 inch of headspace at the top of the jars.

8. Remove Air Bubbles: Use a bubble remover or non-metallic utensil to release any air bubbles by running it along the inside edges of the jars.

9. Wipe Jar Rims: Ensure the jar rims are clean and dry. Wipe them with a clean, damp cloth to remove any residue or stickiness.

10. Apply Lids and Bands: Place sterilized lids on the jars and secure them with bands, tightening them until fingertip tight (not too tight).

11. Prepare Water Bath Canner: Place a rack in the bottom of the water bath canner and fill it with enough water to cover the jars by at least 1 to 2 inches.

12. Heat Water: Bring the water in the canner to a boil.

13. Process Jars: Carefully place the filled jars into the canner using a jar lifter. Ensure the water covers the jars by at least 1 inch.

14. Process Time: Process the jars in the boiling water bath for approximately 10-15 minutes, adjusting processing time based on your altitude.

15. Remove Jars: Once processed, turn off the heat and carefully remove the jars using a jar lifter. Place them on a towel or rack to cool.

16. Cool and Seal: Let the jars cool undisturbed for 12-24 hours. As they cool, you'll hear the lids popping, indicating a proper seal.

17. Check Seals: After cooling, check the jar lids for a proper seal by pressing the center of each lid. If sealed, the lid should not flex or pop.

18. Store the properly sealed jars of jam in a cool, dark place. Use within a year for the best quality. Enjoy your homemade jam spread on toast, biscuits, or as a delightful topping!

Canning Jelly

Ingredients/Equipment:

• Fresh fruits (such as berries, grapes, apples, etc.)

• Granulated sugar

• Pectin (for gelling)

• Water bath canner

• Canning jars, lids, and bands

• Cheesecloth or jelly bag

• Large pot for cooking jelly

• Jar lifter, canning funnel, and ladle

Instructions:

1. Wash and Prepare Fruit: Wash the fruits thoroughly under running water. Remove stems, pits, or any spoiled parts. Chop larger fruits into smaller pieces.

2. Place the prepared fruits in a large pot and crush or mash them to release the juice.

3. Heat the fruit over low to medium heat, stirring occasionally, until the fruits release their juices.

4. Strain Juice: Strain the fruit mixture through a cheesecloth or jelly bag to separate the juice from solids, allowing the juice to drip into a clean container. This helps clarify the juice.

5. Measure Juice: Measure the extracted fruit juice. This measurement will determine the amount of sugar and pectin needed according to the instructions on the pectin package.

6. Cook Juice: Transfer the measured juice to a large pot or saucepan. Bring the juice to a boil over medium-high heat.

7. Add Sugar and Pectin: Gradually add sugar and pectin to the boiling juice according to the package instructions. Stir continuously to dissolve sugar and pectin completely.

8. Boil Jelly Mixture: Increase the heat and bring the juice, sugar, and pectin mixture to a rolling boil that cannot be stirred down. Boil for a specific amount of time specified in the pectin instructions, usually around 1-2 minutes.

9. Test for Gel Point: Perform a gel test by placing a small amount of the boiling jelly mixture on a chilled plate or spoon. Let it cool briefly, then push the edge of the jelly with your finger. If it wrinkles and holds its shape, it has reached the gel point.

10. Prepare Jars: Wash canning jars, lids, and bands in hot, soapy water. Sterilize them by boiling in water for 10 minutes or using a dishwasher's sterilization cycle.

11. Fill Jars: Using a ladle and canning funnel, carefully fill the hot, sterilized jars with the hot jelly mixture, leaving about 1/4 inch of headspace at the top of the jars.

12. Remove Air Bubbles: Use a bubble remover or non-metallic utensil to release any air bubbles by running it along the inside edges of the jars.

13. Wipe Jar Rims: Ensure the jar rims are clean and dry. Wipe them with a clean, damp cloth to remove any residue or stickiness.

14. Apply Lids and Bands: Place sterilized lids on the jars and secure them with bands, tightening them until fingertip tight (not too tight).

15. Prepare Water Bath Canner: Place a rack in the bottom of the water bath canner and fill it with enough water to cover the jars by at least 1 to 2 inches.

16. Heat Water: Bring the water in the canner to a boil.

17. Process Jars: Carefully place the filled jars into the canner using a jar lifter. Ensure the water covers the jars by at least 1 inch.

18. Process Time: Process the jars in the boiling water bath for approximately 5-10 minutes, adjusting processing time based on your altitude.

19. Remove Jars: Once processed, turn off the heat and carefully remove the jars using a jar lifter. Place them on a towel or rack to cool.

20. Cool and Seal: Let the jars cool undisturbed for 12-24 hours. As they cool, you'll hear the lids popping, indicating a proper seal.

21. Check Seals: After cooling, check the jar lids for a proper seal by pressing the center of each lid. If sealed, the lid should not flex or pop.

22. Store the properly sealed jars of jelly in a cool, dark place. Use within a year for the best quality. Enjoy your homemade jelly on toast, pastries, or as a flavorful addition to your favorite dishes!

Canning Fruit Preserves

Ingredients/Equipment:

• Fresh fruits (berries, peaches, apricots, etc.)

• Granulated sugar

• Pectin (optional, for gelling)

• Water bath canner

• Canning jars, lids, and bands

• Large pot for cooking preserves

• Jar lifter, canning funnel, and ladle

Instructions:

1. Wash and Prepare Fruit: Wash the fruits thoroughly under running water. Remove stems, pits, or any spoiled parts. Chop larger fruits into smaller pieces.

2. Mash or Crush Fruit: Crush or mash the prepared fruit in a pot using a potato masher or fork to release juices and create the desired consistency for the preserves.

3. Cook Fruit: Place the mashed fruit in a large pot or saucepan. Cook the fruit over medium heat, stirring occasionally, until it softens and begins to simmer.

4. Add Sugar and Pectin: Gradually add sugar to the fruit, stirring continuously until the sugar dissolves. If using pectin for gelling, follow the manufacturer's instructions and add it to the mixture accordingly.

5. Boil Preserves: Increase the heat to bring the fruit and sugar mixture to a rolling boil. Stir frequently to prevent sticking or burning. Continue boiling until the preserves thicken, reach the desired consistency, and pass the gel test (dropping a small amount on a chilled plate to check for thickness).

6. Prepare Jars: Wash canning jars, lids, and bands in hot, soapy water. Sterilize them by boiling in water for 10 minutes or using a dishwasher's sterilization cycle.

7. Fill Jars: Using a ladle and canning funnel, carefully fill the hot, sterilized jars with the hot preserves, leaving about 1/4 inch of headspace at the top of the jars.

8. Remove Air Bubbles: Use a bubble remover or non-metallic utensil to release any air bubbles by running it along the inside edges of the jars.

9. Wipe Jar Rims: Ensure the jar rims are clean and dry. Wipe them with a clean, damp cloth to remove any residue or stickiness.

10. Apply Lids and Bands: Place sterilized lids on the jars and secure them with bands, tightening them until fingertip tight (not too tight).

11. Prepare Water Bath Canner: Place a rack in the bottom of the water bath canner and fill it with enough water to cover the jars by at least 1 to 2 inches.

12. Heat Water: Bring the water in the canner to a boil.

13. Process Jars: Carefully place the filled jars into the canner using a jar lifter. Ensure the water covers the jars by at least 1 inch.

14. Process Time: Process the jars in the boiling water bath for approximately 10-15 minutes, adjusting processing time based on your altitude.

15. Remove Jars: Once processed, turn off the heat and carefully remove the jars using a jar lifter. Place them on a towel or rack to cool.

16. Cool and Seal: Let the jars cool undisturbed for 12-24 hours. As they cool, you'll hear the lids popping, indicating a proper seal.

17. Check Seals: After cooling, check the jar lids for a proper seal by pressing the center of each lid. If sealed, the lid should not flex or pop.

18. Store the properly sealed jars of fruit preserves in a cool, dark place. Use within a year for the best quality. Enjoy your homemade fruit preserves on toast, with yogurt, or as a flavorful addition to various recipes!

Canning Pickles

Ingredients/Equipment:

• Pickling cucumbers

• Vinegar (5% acidity)

• Pickling salt

• Pickling spices (optional)

• Fresh dill (optional)

• Garlic cloves (optional)

• Water bath canner

• Canning jars, lids, and bands

• Jar lifter, canning funnel, and ladle

Instructions:

1. Wash Cucumbers: Wash the cucumbers thoroughly under running water. Remove any dirt or debris. Trim off the blossom ends of the cucumbers.

2. Slice or Keep Whole: Decide whether you want whole pickles or prefer to slice them. For whole pickles, leave them intact. For sliced pickles, cut them into desired thickness.

3. Prepare Brine: In a large pot, combine vinegar, water, and pickling salt in the ratio specified by your recipe. Bring the brine to a boil, stirring until the salt dissolves completely.

4. Add Flavors (Optional): To enhance flavor, add pickling spices, fresh dill, garlic cloves, or any other preferred pickling ingredients to the brine. Simmer for a few minutes to infuse flavors.

5. Prepare Jars: Wash canning jars, lids, and bands in hot, soapy water. Sterilize them by boiling in water for 10 minutes or using a dishwasher's sterilization cycle.

6. Fill Jars: Using a canning funnel, pack the prepared cucumbers into the sterilized jars, leaving about 1/2 inch of headspace at the top.

7. Add Hot Brine: Carefully pour the hot pickling liquid (brine) over the cucumbers, ensuring the liquid covers the cucumbers while maintaining the recommended headspace.

8. Remove Air Bubbles: Use a bubble remover or non-metallic utensil to release any air bubbles by running it along the inside edges of the jars.

9. Wipe Jar Rims: Ensure the jar rims are clean and dry. Wipe them with a clean, damp cloth to remove any residue or stickiness.

10. Apply Lids and Bands: Place sterilized lids on the jars and secure them with bands, tightening them until fingertip tight (not too tight).

11. Prepare Water Bath Canner: Place a rack in the bottom of the water bath canner and fill it with enough water to cover the jars by at least 1 to 2 inches.

12. Heat Water: Bring the water in the canner to a boil.

13. Process Jars: Carefully place the filled jars into the canner using a jar lifter. Ensure the water covers the jars by at least 1 inch.

14. Process Time: Process the jars in the boiling water bath for approximately 10-15 minutes, adjusting processing time based on your altitude.

15. Remove Jars: Once processed, turn off the heat and carefully remove the jars using a jar lifter. Place them on a towel or rack to cool.

16. Cool and Seal: Let the jars cool undisturbed for 12-24 hours. As they cool, you'll hear the lids popping, indicating a proper seal.

17. Check Seals: After cooling, check the jar lids for a proper seal by pressing the center of each lid. If sealed, the lid should not flex or pop.

18. Store the properly sealed jars of pickles in a cool, dark place. Allow them to sit for a few weeks to develop their flavor before consuming. Enjoy your homemade pickles with sandwiches, salads, or as a tangy snack!

PRESSURE CANNING RECIPES

Canning Beans

Ingredients/Equipment:

- Fresh beans (green beans, snap beans, etc.)

- Pressure canner

- Canning jars, lids, and bands

- Jar lifter, canning funnel, and ladle

- Salt (optional)

Instructions:

1. Wash and Trim Beans: Wash the beans thoroughly under running water. Trim the ends and remove any damaged spots.

2. Cut Beans (Optional): Cut the beans into desired lengths, typically 1-2 inch pieces.

3. Prepare Jars: Wash canning jars, lids, and bands in hot, soapy water. Sterilize them by boiling in water for 10 minutes or using a dishwasher's sterilization cycle.

4. Prepare Brine (Optional): If desired, prepare a brine solution by dissolving salt in water (if using). This step is optional.

5. Fill Jars: Using a canning funnel, pack the prepared beans into the sterilized jars, leaving about 1 inch of headspace at the top.

6. Add Liquid (Optional): Pour boiling water or the prepared brine solution (if using) over the beans, maintaining the recommended headspace.

7. Remove Air Bubbles: Use a bubble remover or non-metallic utensil to release any air bubbles by running it along the inside edges of the jars.

8. Wipe Jar Rims: Ensure the jar rims are clean and dry. Wipe them with a clean, damp cloth to remove any residue or stickiness.

9. Apply Lids and Bands: Place sterilized lids on the jars and secure them with bands, tightening them until fingertip tight (not too tight).

10. Prepare Pressure Canner: Follow the manufacturer's instructions for your specific pressure canner. Add the appropriate amount of water to the canner.

11. Add Jars to Canner: Place the filled jars into the pressure canner using a jar lifter, making sure they're not touching each other and are upright.

12. Secure Lid and Vent Canner: Close the lid of the pressure canner securely. Follow the canner's instructions to vent the canner to release any air inside.

13. Process Jars: Process the jars at the appropriate pressure for the type of beans and your altitude. Consult your pressure canner's manual or reputable canning resources for recommended processing times.

14. Control Pressure: Maintain the recommended pressure by adjusting the heat. Start timing the processing once the correct pressure is reached and stabilized.

15. Complete Processing: After the processing time is completed, turn off the heat. Allow the pressure canner to depressurize naturally.

16. Remove Jars: Carefully open the canner lid away from your face. Use a jar lifter to remove the jars and place them on a towel or rack to cool.

17. Cool and Check Seals: Let the jars cool undisturbed for 12-24 hours. Check the lids for proper sealing by pressing the center of each lid. If sealed, the lid should not flex or pop.

18. Store the properly sealed jars of beans in a cool, dark place. Use within a year for the best quality. Enjoy your home-canned beans in soups, salads, or as a nutritious side dish!

Canning Corn

Ingredients/Equipment:

• Fresh corn on the cob

• Pressure canner

• Canning jars, lids, and bands

• Jar lifter, canning funnel, and ladle

• Salt (optional)

Instructions:

1. Select Fresh Corn: Choose fresh, tender corn on the cob. Husk the corn and remove silk.

2. Blanch Corn (Optional): To help retain quality during canning, blanch the corn in boiling water for about 4-5 minutes, then immediately place it in ice water to stop the cooking process.

3. Cut Corn from Cob (Optional): After blanching, if desired, cut the corn kernels from the cob. Use a sharp knife and slide it down the cob to remove the kernels.

4. Prepare Jars: Wash canning jars, lids, and bands in hot, soapy water. Sterilize them by boiling in water for 10 minutes or using a dishwasher's sterilization cycle.

5. Fill Jars with Corn: Pack the prepared corn kernels or whole cobs tightly into the sterilized jars, leaving about 1 inch of headspace at the top of the jars.

6. Add Salt (Optional): If desired, add a teaspoon of salt per quart jar. This step is optional.

7. Wipe Jar Rims: Ensure the jar rims are clean and dry. Wipe them with a clean, damp cloth to remove any residue or stickiness.

8. Apply Lids and Bands: Place sterilized lids on the jars and secure them with bands, tightening them until fingertip tight (not too tight).

9. Prepare Pressure Canner: Follow the manufacturer's instructions for your specific pressure canner. Add the appropriate amount of water to the canner.

10. Add Jars to Canner: Place the filled jars into the pressure canner using a jar lifter, making sure they're not touching each other and are upright.

11. Secure Lid and Vent Canner: Close the lid of the pressure canner securely. Follow the canner's instructions to vent the canner to release any air inside.

12. Process Jars: Process the jars at the appropriate pressure for your altitude and the type of corn being canned. Consult reliable canning resources for recommended processing times.

13. Control Pressure: Maintain the recommended pressure by adjusting the heat. Start timing the processing once the correct pressure is reached and stabilized.

14. Complete Processing: After the processing time is completed, turn off the heat. Allow the pressure canner to depressurize naturally.

15. Remove Jars: Carefully open the canner lid away from your face. Use a jar lifter to remove the jars and place them on a towel or rack to cool.

16. Cool and Check Seals: Let the jars cool undisturbed for 12-24 hours. Check the lids for proper sealing by pressing the center of each lid. If sealed, the lid should not flex or pop.

17. Store the properly sealed jars of corn in a cool, dark place. Use within a year for the best quality. Enjoy your home-canned corn in soups, casseroles, or as a delicious side dish!

Canning Carrots

Ingredients/Equipment:

• Fresh carrots

• Pressure canner

• Canning jars, lids, and bands

• Jar lifter, canning funnel, and ladle

• Salt (optional)

Instructions:

1. Wash and Peel Carrots: Scrub the carrots under running water to remove dirt. Peel the carrots and trim off any blemishes or damaged spots.

2. Cut Carrots: Cut the carrots into desired sizes - typically, slices, sticks, or small chunks.

3. Prepare Jars: Wash canning jars, lids, and bands in hot, soapy water. Sterilize them by boiling in water for 10 minutes or using a dishwasher's sterilization cycle.

4. Fill Jars with Carrots: Pack the prepared carrots into the sterilized jars, leaving about 1 inch of headspace at the top of the jars.

5. Add Salt (Optional): If desired, add a teaspoon of salt per quart jar. This step is optional.

6. Wipe Jar Rims: Ensure the jar rims are clean and dry. Wipe them with a clean, damp cloth to remove any residue or stickiness.

7. Apply Lids and Bands: Place sterilized lids on the jars and secure them with bands, tightening them until fingertip tight (not too tight).

8. Prepare Pressure Canner: Follow the manufacturer's instructions for your specific pressure canner. Add the appropriate amount of water to the canner.

9. Add Jars to Canner: Place the filled jars into the pressure canner using a jar lifter, making sure they're not touching each other and are upright.

10. Secure Lid and Vent Canner: Close the lid of the pressure canner securely. Follow the canner's instructions to vent the canner to release any air inside.

11. Process Jars: Process the jars at the appropriate pressure for your altitude and the type of carrots being canned. Consult reliable canning resources for recommended processing times.

12. Control Pressure: Maintain the recommended pressure by adjusting the heat. Start timing the processing once the correct pressure is reached and stabilized.

13. Complete Processing: After the processing time is completed, turn off the heat. Allow the pressure canner to depressurize naturally.

14. Remove Jars: Carefully open the canner lid away from your face. Use a jar lifter to remove the jars and place them on a towel or rack to cool.

15. Cool and Check Seals: Let the jars cool undisturbed for 12-24 hours. Check the lids for proper sealing by pressing the center of each lid. If sealed, the lid should not flex or pop.

16. Store the properly sealed jars of carrots in a cool, dark place. Use within a year for the best quality. Enjoy your home-canned carrots in stews, soups, salads, or as a nutritious side dish!

Canning Mixed Vegetables

Ingredients/Equipment:

• Assorted fresh vegetables (such as carrots, green beans, corn, peas, etc.)

• Pressure canner

• Canning jars, lids, and bands

• Jar lifter, canning funnel, and ladle

• Salt (optional)

Instructions:

1. Wash and Prepare Vegetables: Wash all vegetables thoroughly under running water. Peel, trim, and cut them into uniform sizes, depending on your preference (chunks, slices, etc.).

2. Blanch Vegetables (Optional): To help retain quality during canning, blanch denser vegetables like carrots, beans, and corn in boiling water for a few

minutes, then immediately place them in ice water to stop the cooking process. Softer vegetables like peas might not need blanching.

3. Prepare Jars: Wash canning jars, lids, and bands in hot, soapy water. Sterilize them by boiling in water for 10 minutes or using a dishwasher's sterilization cycle.

4. Fill Jars with Vegetables: Pack the prepared vegetables into the sterilized jars, mixing them as desired to create the mixed vegetable combination. Leave about 1 inch of headspace at the top of the jars.

5. Add Salt (Optional): If desired, add a teaspoon of salt per quart jar. This step is optional.

6. Wipe Jar Rims: Ensure the jar rims are clean and dry. Wipe them with a clean, damp cloth to remove any residue or stickiness.

7. Apply Lids and Bands: Place sterilized lids on the jars and secure them with bands, tightening them until fingertip tight (not too tight).

8. Prepare Pressure Canner: Follow the manufacturer's instructions for your specific pressure canner. Add the appropriate amount of water to the canner.

9. Add Jars to Canner: Place the filled jars into the pressure canner using a jar lifter, ensuring they're not touching each other and are upright.

10. Secure Lid and Vent Canner: Close the lid of the pressure canner securely. Follow the canner's instructions to vent the canner to release any air inside.

11. Process Jars: Process the jars at the appropriate pressure for your altitude and the type of vegetables being canned. Consult reliable canning resources for recommended processing times.

12. Control Pressure: Maintain the recommended pressure by adjusting the heat. Start timing the processing once the correct pressure is reached and stabilized.

13. Complete Processing: After the processing time is completed, turn off the heat. Allow the pressure canner to depressurize naturally.

14. Remove Jars: Carefully open the canner lid away from your face. Use a jar lifter to remove the jars and place them on a towel or rack to cool.

15. Cool and Check Seals: Let the jars cool undisturbed for 12-24 hours. Check the lids for proper sealing by pressing the center of each lid. If sealed, the lid should not flex or pop.

16. Store the properly sealed jars of mixed vegetables in a cool, dark place. Use within a year for the best quality. Enjoy your home-canned mixed vegetables in various dishes and recipes!

Canning Beef

Ingredients/Equipment:

• Fresh beef (cut into chunks or cubes)

• Pressure canner

- Canning jars, lids, and bands

- Jar lifter, canning funnel, and ladle

- Salt (optional)

Instructions:

1. Select and Cut Beef: Choose fresh, high-quality beef with minimal fat. Trim excess fat and cut the beef into uniform chunks or cubes, about 1-inch in size.

2. Pre-cook (Optional): Brown the beef chunks in a pan to enhance flavor, but this step is optional.

3. Prepare Jars: Wash canning jars, lids, and bands in hot, soapy water. Sterilize them by boiling in water for 10 minutes or using a dishwasher's sterilization cycle.

4. Fill Jars with Beef: Pack the prepared beef into the sterilized jars, leaving about 1 inch of headspace at the top.

5. Add Salt (Optional): If desired, add a teaspoon of salt per quart jar. This step is optional.

6. Wipe Jar Rims: Ensure the jar rims are clean and dry. Wipe them with a clean, damp cloth to remove any residue or stickiness.

7. Apply Lids and Bands: Place sterilized lids on the jars and secure them with bands, tightening them until fingertip tight (not too tight).

8. Prepare Pressure Canner: Follow the manufacturer's instructions for your specific pressure canner. Add the appropriate amount of water to the canner.

9. Add Jars to Canner: Place the filled jars into the pressure canner using a jar lifter, ensuring they're not touching each other and are upright.

10. Secure Lid and Vent Canner: Close the lid of the pressure canner securely. Follow the canner's instructions to vent the canner to release any air inside.

11. Process Jars: Process the jars at the appropriate pressure for your altitude and the type of beef being canned. Consult reliable canning resources for recommended processing times.

12. Control Pressure: Maintain the recommended pressure by adjusting the heat. Start timing the processing once the correct pressure is reached and stabilized.

13. Complete Processing: After the processing time is completed, turn off the heat. Allow the pressure canner to depressurize naturally.

14. Remove Jars: Carefully open the canner lid away from your face. Use a jar lifter to remove the jars and place them on a towel or rack to cool.

15. Cool and Check Seals: Let the jars cool undisturbed for 12-24 hours. Check the lids for proper sealing by pressing the center of each lid. If sealed, the lid should not flex or pop.

16. Store the properly sealed jars of beef in a cool, dark place. Use within a year for the best quality. Enjoy your home-canned beef in stews, soups, sandwiches, or other recipes!

Canning Pork

Ingredients/Equipment:

• Fresh pork (cut into chunks or cubes)

• Pressure canner

• Canning jars, lids, and bands

• Jar lifter, canning funnel, and ladle

• Salt (optional)

Instructions:

1. Select and Cut Pork: Choose fresh pork with minimal fat. Trim excess fat and cut the pork into uniform chunks or cubes, approximately 1-inch in size.

2. Pre-cook (Optional): Brown the pork chunks in a pan to enhance flavor, but this step is optional.

3. Prepare Jars: Wash canning jars, lids, and bands in hot, soapy water. Sterilize them by boiling in water for 10 minutes or using a dishwasher's sterilization cycle.

4. Fill Jars with Pork: Pack the prepared pork into the sterilized jars, leaving about 1 inch of headspace at the top.

5. Add Salt (Optional): If desired, add a teaspoon of salt per quart jar. This step is optional.

6. Wipe Jar Rims: Ensure the jar rims are clean and dry. Wipe them with a clean, damp cloth to remove any residue or stickiness.

7. Apply Lids and Bands: Place sterilized lids on the jars and secure them with bands, tightening them until fingertip tight (not too tight).

8. Prepare Pressure Canner: Follow the manufacturer's instructions for your specific pressure canner. Add the appropriate amount of water to the canner.

9. Add Jars to Canner: Place the filled jars into the pressure canner using a jar lifter, ensuring they're not touching each other and are upright.

10. Secure Lid and Vent Canner: Close the lid of the pressure canner securely. Follow the canner's instructions to vent the canner to release any air inside.

11. Process Jars: Process the jars at the appropriate pressure for your altitude and the type of pork being canned. Consult reliable canning resources for recommended processing times.

12. Control Pressure: Maintain the recommended pressure by adjusting the heat. Start timing the processing once the correct pressure is reached and stabilized.

13. Complete Processing: After the processing time is completed, turn off the heat. Allow the pressure canner to depressurize naturally.

14. Remove Jars: Carefully open the canner lid away from your face. Use a jar lifter to remove the jars and place them on a towel or rack to cool.

15. Cool and Check Seals: Let the jars cool undisturbed for 12-24 hours. Check the lids for proper sealing by pressing the center of each lid. If sealed, the lid should not flex or pop.

16. Store the properly sealed jars of pork in a cool, dark place. Use within a year for the best quality. Enjoy your home-canned pork in various recipes!

Canning Chicken

Ingredients/Equipment:

• Fresh chicken (boneless or bone-in, cut into chunks or cubes)

• Pressure canner

• Canning jars, lids, and bands

• Jar lifter, canning funnel, and ladle

• Salt (optional)

Instructions:

1. Select and Cut Chicken: Choose fresh chicken and remove excess skin and fat. Cut the chicken into uniform chunks or cubes, approximately 1-inch in size.

2. Pre-cook (Optional): Brown the chicken chunks in a pan to enhance flavor, but this step is optional.

3. Prepare Jars: Wash canning jars, lids, and bands in hot, soapy water. Sterilize them by boiling in water for 10 minutes or using a dishwasher's sterilization cycle.

4. Fill Jars with Chicken: Pack the prepared chicken into the sterilized jars, leaving about 1 inch of headspace at the top.

5. Add Salt (Optional): If desired, add a teaspoon of salt per quart jar. This step is optional.

6. Wipe Jar Rims: Ensure the jar rims are clean and dry. Wipe them with a clean, damp cloth to remove any residue or stickiness.

7. Apply Lids and Bands: Place sterilized lids on the jars and secure them with bands, tightening them until fingertip tight (not too tight).

8. Prepare Pressure Canner: Follow the manufacturer's instructions for your specific pressure canner. Add the appropriate amount of water to the canner.

9. Add Jars to Canner: Place the filled jars into the pressure canner using a jar lifter, ensuring they're not touching each other and are upright.

10. Secure Lid and Vent Canner: Close the lid of the pressure canner securely. Follow the canner's instructions to vent the canner to release any air inside.

11. Process Jars: Process the jars at the appropriate pressure for your altitude and the type of chicken being canned. Consult reliable canning resources for recommended processing times.

12. Control Pressure: Maintain the recommended pressure by adjusting the heat. Start timing the processing once the correct pressure is reached and stabilized.

13. Complete Processing: After the processing time is completed, turn off the heat. Allow the pressure canner to depressurize naturally.

14. Remove Jars: Carefully open the canner lid away from your face. Use a jar lifter to remove the jars and place them on a towel or rack to cool.

15. Cool and Check Seals: Let the jars cool undisturbed for 12-24 hours. Check the lids for proper sealing by pressing the center of each lid. If sealed, the lid should not flex or pop.

16. Store the properly sealed jars of chicken in a cool, dark place. Use within a year for the best quality. Enjoy your home-canned chicken in soups, stews, sandwiches, and other recipes!

Canning Fish

Ingredients/Equipment:

• Fresh fish fillets or chunks (salmon, tuna, mackerel, etc.)

• Pressure canner

- Canning jars, lids, and bands

- Jar lifter, canning funnel, and ladle

- Salt (optional)

Instructions:

1. Select and Clean Fish: Choose fresh, high-quality fish. Remove scales, skin, and bones. Rinse the fish thoroughly under cold water and cut into suitable-sized pieces.

2. Pre-cook (Optional): You can pre-cook the fish by poaching or baking. This step is optional but can improve texture and flavor.

3. Prepare Jars: Wash canning jars, lids, and bands in hot, soapy water. Sterilize them by boiling in water for 10 minutes or using a dishwasher's sterilization cycle.

4. Fill Jars with Fish: Pack the prepared fish into the sterilized jars, leaving about 1 inch of headspace at the top.

5. Add Salt (Optional): If desired, add a teaspoon of salt per quart jar. This step is optional.

6. Wipe Jar Rims: Ensure the jar rims are clean and dry. Wipe them with a clean, damp cloth to remove any residue or stickiness.

7. Apply Lids and Bands: Place sterilized lids on the jars and secure them with bands, tightening them until fingertip tight (not too tight).

8. Prepare Pressure Canner: Follow the manufacturer's instructions for your specific pressure canner. Add the appropriate amount of water to the canner.

9. Add Jars to Canner: Place the filled jars into the pressure canner using a jar lifter, ensuring they're not touching each other and are upright.

10. Secure Lid and Vent Canner: Close the lid of the pressure canner securely. Follow the canner's instructions to vent the canner to release any air inside.

11. Process Jars: Process the jars at the appropriate pressure for your altitude and the type of fish being canned. Consult reliable canning resources for recommended processing times.

12. Control Pressure: Maintain the recommended pressure by adjusting the heat. Start timing the processing once the correct pressure is reached and stabilized.

13. Complete Processing: After the processing time is completed, turn off the heat. Allow the pressure canner to depressurize naturally.

14. Remove Jars: Carefully open the canner lid away from your face. Use a jar lifter to remove the jars and place them on a towel or rack to cool.

15. Cool and Check Seals: Let the jars cool undisturbed for 12-24 hours. Check the lids for proper sealing by pressing the center of each lid. If sealed, the lid should not flex or pop.

16. Store the properly sealed jars of fish in a cool, dark place. Use within a year for the best quality. Enjoy your home-canned fish in salads, sandwiches, or as a main course!

Canning Soups

Ingredients/Equipment:

• Ingredients for various soup (vegetables, meats, broth, seasonings, etc.)

• Pressure canner

• Canning jars, lids, and bands

• Jar lifter, canning funnel, and ladle

Instructions:

1. Choose Soup Recipes: Select different soup recipes that you'd like to can. This could include vegetable soup, chicken noodle soup, beef stew, minestrone, and lentil soup, for example.

2. Prepare Soup Ingredients: Follow each soup recipe, prepare the ingredients, chop vegetables, cook meats if necessary, and simmer them in their respective broths or liquids.

3. Prepare Jars: Wash canning jars, lids, and bands in hot, soapy water. Sterilize them by boiling in water for 10 minutes or using a dishwasher's sterilization cycle.

4. Fill Jars with Soups: Ladle the hot soups into the sterilized jars, leaving about 1 to 1.5 inches of headspace at the top.

5. Wipe Jar Rims: Ensure the jar rims are clean and dry. Wipe them with a clean, damp cloth to remove any residue or stickiness.

6. Apply Lids and Bands: Place sterilized lids on the jars and secure them with bands, tightening them until fingertip tight (not too tight).

7. Prepare Pressure Canner: Follow the manufacturer's instructions for your specific pressure canner. Add the appropriate amount of water to the canner.

8. Add Jars to Canner: Place the filled jars into the pressure canner using a jar lifter, ensuring they're not touching each other and are upright.

9. Secure Lid and Vent Canner: Close the lid of the pressure canner securely. Follow the canner's instructions to vent the canner to release any air inside.

10. Process Jars: Process the jars at the appropriate pressure for your altitude and the type of soups being canned. Consult reliable canning resources for recommended processing times specific to each soup type.

11. Control Pressure: Maintain the recommended pressure by adjusting the heat. Start timing the processing once the correct pressure is reached and stabilized.

12. Complete Processing: After the processing time is completed, turn off the heat. Allow the pressure canner to depressurize naturally.

13. Remove Jars: Carefully open the canner lid away from your face. Use a jar lifter to remove the jars and place them on a towel or rack to cool.

14. Cool and Check Seals: Let the jars cool undisturbed for 12-24 hours. Check the lids for proper sealing by pressing the center of each lid. If sealed, the lid should not flex or pop.

15. Store the properly sealed jars of soups in a cool, dark place. Label the jars with the soup type and date canned. Use within a year for the best quality. Enjoy your home-canned soups whenever you desire a warm, comforting meal!

CONCLUSION

Home canning and preserving offer a wealth of opportunities to extend the life of seasonal produce, meats, and soups, allowing you to savor their freshness and flavors long after their harvest or creation. Through various methods such as water bath canning, pressure canning, freezing, dehydrating, and smoking, a diverse range of foods can be preserved, including fruits, vegetables, meats, and soups.

While the canning process involves meticulous attention to cleanliness, proper equipment, and adherence to safety guidelines, the end result yields an array of nutritious, flavorful, and convenient options for meals throughout the year. Whether enjoying the vibrancy of freshly preserved fruits, the hearty satisfaction of canned vegetables, or the convenience of ready-to-eat canned soups and meats, home-canned foods reflect dedication, skill, and a desire for quality.

Additionally, proper labeling, storage, and rotation are crucial elements in maintaining the integrity and safety of home-canned goods. By following recommended procedures, noting the contents and dates on labels, and storing jars in a cool, dark environment, the quality and safety of preserved foods can be maximized.

Ultimately, embracing the art of home canning and preserving not only fosters self-sufficiency but also connects us to traditional methods of food preservation while ensuring the availability of flavorful, nutritious foods throughout the year. Whether cherishing the taste of summer fruits in the depths of winter or relishing the comfort of a homemade soup, the rewards of home preservation extend far beyond the process itself, enriching our meals and memories with the bounty of each season.

Made in the USA
Columbia, SC
02 January 2024

29778665R00054